To: _____

From: _____

Also by Jim Reimann

Streams in the Desert: 366 Daily Devotional Readings (by L. B. Cowman)

My Utmost for His Highest: An Updated Edition in Today's Language (by Oswald Chambers)

Look Unto Me: The Devotions of Charles Spurgeon Expanded, Indexed, and Updated

Hear My Voice: The Devotions of Charles Spurgeon Expanded, Indexed, and Updated (coming Fall 2010)

streams for teens

THOUGHTS ON SEEKING GOD'S WILL AND DIRECTION

30 DEVOTIONS FROM *STREAMS IN THE DESERT®*

l.b. cowman, edited by

jim reimann

editor of *streams in the desert®*
and *my utmost for his highest*, updated editions

ZONDERVAN®

ZONDERVAN.com/
AUTHORTRACKER
follow your favorite authors

Streams for Teens
Copyright © 2009 by Zondervan

Requests for information should be addressed to:

Zondervan, *Grand Rapids, Michigan 49530*

ISBN 978-0-310-28311-9

Interior design by Christine Orejuela-Winkelman

Printed in China

08 09 10 11 12 13 14 • 18 17 16 15 14 13 12 11 10 9 8 7 6 5 4 3 2 1

Contents

Introduction

Why read this little book?

As a teenager your life is about to change in ways you could never imagine. Opportunities will cross your path and various decisions will need to be made. Which way will you turn? What will be the focus of your adult life? Who will you serve? What will be your purpose? Will you make a difference in this world?

This little book is comprised of thirty specially selected devotions from Streams in the Desert, each chosen to help you answer those questions from a Christian perspective. They are Bible-based, and, therefore, can be trusted to help you plan your future. They will help you find God's will at a time in your life when that can be a confusing thing. Yet if you will commit your life to the truths in this little book, your life will be focused on God's path of blessing for you.

My role has been to update the language of these devotions, since some of the quotes are nearly five hundred years old. They were originally compiled by Lettie Cowman who was a pioneer missionary to Japan and China from 1901 to 1917, along with her husband, Charles. These devotions, first published in 1925, have endured because they have the power of God's Word in them. Not only have I updated them, but I also have applied these truths to my own life, and can testify to their life-guiding principles.

May the Lord bless you as you embark on a new phase of your life, and may you entrust your walk to the Lord who promised:

Whether you turn to the right or to the left, your ears will hear a voice behind you, saying, "This is the way; walk in it." (Isaiah. 30:21)

Jim Reimann

Editor of the updated editions of:
Streams in the Desert
My Utmost for His Highest
Look Unto Me: *The Devotions of Charles Spurgeon*
Hear My Voice: The Devotions of
Charles Spurgeon, coming Fall 2010

streams for teens

Your Sovereign God Who Guides

Paul and his companions ... [were] kept by
the Holy Spirit from preaching the word in
the province of Asia.

Acts 16:6

It is interesting to study the way God extended His guidance to these early messengers of the Cross. It consisted mainly in prohibiting their movement when they attempted to take a course other than the right one. When they wanted to turn to the left, toward Asia, He stopped them. When they sought to turn to the right, toward Bithynia in Asia Minor, He stopped them again. In his later years, Paul would do some of his greatest work in that very region, yet now the door was closed before him by the Holy Spirit. The time was not yet ripe for the attack on these apparently impregnable bastions of the kingdom of Satan. Apollos needed to go there first to lay the groundwork. Paul and Barnabas were needed more urgently elsewhere and required further training before undertaking this responsible task.

Beloved, whenever you are in doubt as to which way to turn, submit your judgment absolutely to the Spirit of God, asking Him to shut every door but the right one. Say to Him, "Blessed Spirit, I give to You the entire responsibility of closing every road and stopping every step that is not of God. Let me hear Your voice behind me whenever I turn aside to the right or to the left" (Deut. 5:32).

In the meantime, continue along the path you have already been traveling. Persist in your calling until you are clearly told to do something else. O traveler, the Spirit of Jesus is waiting to be to you what He was to Paul. Just be careful to obey even His smallest nudging or warning. Then after you have prayed the prayer of faith and there are no apparent hindrances, go forward with a confident heart. Do not be surprised if your answer comes in doors closing before you. But when doors are shut to the right and left, an open road is sure to lead to Troas. Luke waits for you there, and visions will point the way to where vast opportunities remain open, and faithful friends are waiting. *from Paul, by F. B. Meyer.*

> Is there some problem in your life to solve,
> Some passage seeming full of mystery?

God knows, who brings the hidden things
to light.
He keeps the key.

Is there some door closed by the Father's
hand
Which widely opened you had hoped to see?
Trust God and wait—for when He shuts the
door
He keeps the key.

Is there some earnest prayer unanswered
yet,
Or answered NOT as you had thought
'twould be?
God will make clear His purpose by and by.
He keeps the key.

Have patience with your God, your patient
God,
All wise, all knowing, no long lingerer He,
And of the door of all your future life
He keeps the key.

Unfailing comfort, sweet and blessed rest,
To know of EVERY door He keeps the key.
That He at last when just HE sees is best,
Will give it THEE.

Anonymous

Your Sovereign God Who Leads

> When he has brought out all his own,
> he goes on ahead of them.
>
> John 10:4

This is intensely difficult work for Him and us—it is difficult for us to go, but equally difficult for Him to cause us pain. Yet it must be done. It would not be in our best interest to always remain in one happy and comfortable location. Therefore He moves us forward. The shepherd leaves the fold so the sheep will move on to the vitalizing mountain slopes. In the same way, laborers must be driven out into the harvest, or else the golden grain would spoil.

But take heart! It could never be better to stay once He determines otherwise; if the loving hand of our Lord moves us forward, it must be best. Forward, in His name, to green pastures, quiet waters, and mountain heights! (See Psalm 23:2.) *He goes on ahead of [us].* So whatever awaits us is encountered first by Him, and the eye of faith can always discern His majestic presence out in front. When His presence cannot be seen, it is dangerous to move ahead. Comfort your heart with the fact that the Savior has Himself experienced all the trials He asks you to endure; He would not ask you to pass through them unless He was sure that the paths were not too difficult or strenuous for you.

This is the blessed life—not anxious to see far down the road nor overly concerned about the next step, not eager to choose the path nor weighted down with the heavy responsibilities of the future, but quietly following the Shepherd, *one step at a time.*

> Dark is the sky! and veiled the unknown
> morrow!
> Dark is life's way, for night is not yet o'er;
> The longed-for glimpse I may not
> meanwhile borrow;
> But, this I know and trust, HE GOES BEFORE.
>
> Dangers are near! and fears my mind are
> shaking;
> Heart seems to dread what life may hold in
> store;
> But I am His—He knows the way I'm
> taking,
> More blessed even still—HE GOES BEFORE.

Doubts cast their weird, unwelcome
                 shadows o'er me,
Doubts that life's best—life's choicest
                 things are o'er;
What but His Word can strengthen, can
                 restore me,
And this blest fact; that still HE GOES
                 BEFORE.

HE GOES BEFORE! Be this my consolation!
He goes before! On this my heart would
                 dwell!
He goes before! This guarantees salvation!
HE GOES BEFORE! And therefore all is well.

                 J. Danson Smith

The oriental shepherd always walked *ahead* of his sheep. He was always *out in front.* Any attack upon the sheep had to take him into account first. Now God is out in front. He is in our tomorrows, and it is tomorrow that fills people with fear. *Yet God is already there.* All the tomorrows of our life have to pass through Him before they can get to us. *F. B. Meyer*

God is in every tomorrow,
   Therefore I live for today,
Certain of finding at sunrise,

Guidance and strength for my way;
Power for each moment of weakness,
Hope for each moment of pain,
Comfort for every sorrow,
Sunshine and joy after rain.

Your God — The Living God

Daniel, servant of the living God, has your God,
whom you serve continually, been able
to rescue you from the lions?

Daniel 6:20

We find the expression *the living God* many times in the Scriptures, and yet it is the very thing we are so prone to forget. We know it is written *the living God,* but in our daily life there is almost nothing we lose sight of as often as the fact that God is *the living God.* We forget that He is now exactly what He was three or four thousand years ago, that He has the same sovereign power, and that He extends the same gracious love toward those who love and serve Him. We overlook the fact that He will do for us now what He did thousands of years ago for others, simply because He is the unchanging, *living God.* What a great reason to confide in Him, and in our darkest moments to never lose sight of the fact that He *is* still, and ever will be, *the living God*!

Be assured, if you walk with Him, look to Him, and expect help from Him, He will never fail you. An older believer who has known the Lord for forty-four years wrote the following as an encouragement to you: "God has never failed me. Even in my greatest difficulties, heaviest trials, and deepest poverty and need, He has never failed me. Because I was enabled by God's grace to trust Him, He has always come to my aid. I delight in speaking well of His name." *George Mueller*

Martin Luther, deep in thought and needing to grasp hidden strength during a time of danger and fear in his life, was seen tracing on the table with his finger the words "He lives! He lives!" This is our hope for ourselves, His truth, and humankind. People come and go. Leaders, teachers, and philosophers speak and work for a season and then fall silent and powerless. He abides. They die but He lives. They are lights that glow yet are ultimately extinguished. But He is the true Light from which they draw their brightness, and He shines forevermore. *Alexander Maclaren*

"One day I came to know Dr. John Douglas Adam," wrote Charles Gallaudet Trumbull. "I learned he considered his greatest spiritual asset to be his *unwavering awareness of the actual presence of Jesus.* Nothing sustained him as much, he said, as the realization that Jesus was *always* actually present with him. This realization was totally independent of his own feelings, his worthiness, and his perceptions as to how Jesus would demonstrate His presence.

"Furthermore, he said Christ was the center of his thoughts. Whenever his mind was free from other matters, it would turn to Christ. Whenever he was alone, and no matter where he was, he would talk aloud to Christ as easily and as naturally as to any human friend. That is how very real Jesus' *actual presence* was to him."

Willing to Be Great—
But Unknown

Though John never performed a miraculous sign,
all that John said about this man was true.

John 10:41

Perhaps you are very dissatisfied with yourself.
You are not a genius, have no distinctive gifts, and
are inconspicuous when it comes to having any special
abilities. Mediocrity seems to be the measure of your
existence. None of your days are noteworthy, except
for their sameness and lack of zest. Yet in spite of this,
you may live a great life.

John the Baptist never performed a miracle, but
Jesus said of him, "Among those born of women there
is no one greater" (Luke 7:28). His mission was to be
"a witness to the light" (John 1:8), and that may be
your mission and mine. John was content to be only a
voice, if it caused people to think of Christ.

Be willing to be only a voice that is heard but not seen, or a mirror whose glass the eye cannot see because it is reflecting the brilliant glory of the Son. Be willing to be a breeze that arises just before daylight, saying, "The dawn! The dawn!" and then fades away.

Do the most everyday, even at insignificant tasks, knowing that God can see. If you live with difficult people, win them over through love. If you once made a great mistake in life, do not allow it to cloud the rest of your life, but by locking it secretly in your heart, make it yield strength and character.

We are doing more good than we know. The things we do today—sowing seeds or sharing simple truths of Christ—people will someday refer to as the first things that prompted them to think of Him. For my part, I will be satisfied not to have some great tombstone over my grave, but just to know that common people will gather there once I am gone and say, "He was a good man. He never performed any miracles, but he told me about Christ, which led me to know Him for myself." *George Matheson*

Thy Hidden Ones (Psalm 83:3 KJV)

Thick green leaves from the soft brown
earth,
Happy springtime has called them forth;
First faint promise of summer bloom
Breathes from the fragrant, sweet perfume,
Under the leaves.

Lift them! what marvelous beauty lies
Hidden beneath, from our thoughtless eyes!
Mayflowers, rosy or purest white,
Lift their cups to the sudden light,
Under the leaves.

Are there no lives whose holy deeds —
Seen by no eye save His who reads
Motive and action — in silence grow
Into rare beauty, and bud and blow
Under the leaves?

Fair white flowers of faith and trust,
Springing from spirits bruised and crushed;
Blossoms of love, rose-tinted and bright,
Touched and painted with Heaven's own
light
Under the leaves.

Full fresh clusters of duty borne,
Fairest of all in that shadow grown;
Wondrous the fragrance that sweet and rare
Comes from the flower-cups hidden there
    Under the leaves.

Though unseen by our vision dim,
Bud and blossom are known to Him;
Wait we content for His heavenly ray—
Wait till our Master Himself one day
    Lifts up the leaves.

God calls many of His most valued workers from the unknown multitude. (See Luke 14:23.)

Setting Sail into the Deep

> Put out into deep water.
>
> Luke 5:4

The Lord did not say how deep. The depth of the water into which we sail depends upon how completely we have cut our ties to the shore, the greatness of our need, and our anxieties about the future. Yet the fish were to be found in the deep, not the shallow, water.

It is the same with us—our needs are to be met in the deep things of God. We are to sail into the deep of God's Word, which the Holy Spirit will open to us with profound yet crystal-clear meaning. And the words we knew in the past will have an ocean of new meaning, which will render their original message very shallow.

"Put out into [the] deep" of the atonement. We must continue until the Spirit brings such understanding of Christ's precious blood that it becomes an omnipotent balm, food, and medicine for our soul and body.

"Put out into [the] deep" of the Father's will. We must endure until we fully comprehend its infinite detail and goodness and its far-reaching provision and care for us.

"Put out into [the] deep" of the Holy Spirit. We must never stop until He becomes to us a warm, shining, radiant, and fathomless sea, one in which we soak, basking and breathing and ultimately losing ourselves and our sorrows in the calmness and peace of His everlasting presence. We must keep on until the Spirit becomes a clear and glorious answer to our prayer; our most careful and tender guide; the most thoughtful anticipator of our needs; and the most skilled and supernatural sculptor of our circumstances.

"Put out into [the] deep" of God's purposes and His coming kingdom. We must carry on until the Lord's coming and His millennial reign are before us, where we see eternity unfolding beyond the glorious gates, until our imagination is blinded by the brilliant light, and our heart flutters with an inexpressible anticipation of the joy of seeing Jesus and "the glory that will be revealed in us" (Romans 8:18).

Jesus instructs us to set sail into all of these. He created us, and He created the depths of the fathomless sea. And He has made those depths fit together in perfect harmony with all our talents and desires. *from Soul Food*

> Its streams the whole creation reach,
>   So plenteous is the store;
> Enough for all, enough for each;
>   Enough forevermore.

The deep waters of the Holy Spirit are always accessible, because they are always *flowing.* Will you claim afresh and anew today to be immersed and drenched in these waters of life? The waters in Ezekiel's vision were at first "coming out from under the threshold of the temple" (Ezekiel 47:1). Then as a man went to measure it, he found it to be ankle-deep. Soon he measured and found the water was knee-deep. Again he measured and the water was to the waist. Next it was "a river that I could not cross" (Ezekiel 47:5).

How far have we advanced into this river of life? The Holy Spirit desires that our *self* be completely submerged—not merely ankle-deep, knee-deep, waist-deep, but self-deep. He wants us hidden and bathed under this life-giving stream. Let loose the lines holding you to the shore and sail into the deep. And never forget, the Man who does the measuring is with us today. *J. Gresham Machen*

Being Prepared to See Him

I consider that our present sufferings
are not worth comparing with the glory
that will be revealed in us.

Romans 8:18

A remarkable event occurred recently at a wedding in England. The bridegroom, a very wealthy young man of high social standing, had been blinded by an accident at the age of ten. In spite of his blindness, he had graduated from the university with honors and had now won the heart of his beautiful bride, although he had never looked upon her face. Shortly before his marriage he underwent a new round of treatments by specialists, and the result was ready to be revealed on the day of his wedding.

The big day arrived, with all the guests and their presents. In attendance were cabinet ministers, generals, bishops, and learned men and women. The groom, dressed for the wedding but with his eyes still covered by bandages, rode to the church with his father. His famous ophthalmologist met them in the vestry of the church.

The bride entered the church on the arm of her white-haired father. She was so moved, she could hardly speak. Would the man she loved finally see her face—a face others admired but he knew only through the touch of his delicate fingertips?

As she neared the altar, while the soft strains of the wedding march floated through the church, she saw an unusual group. There before her stood the groom, his father, and the doctor. The doctor was in the process of cutting away the last bandage.

Once the bandage was removed, the groom took a step forward, yet with the trembling uncertainty of someone who is not completely awake. A beam of rose-colored light from a pane in the window above the altar fell across his face, but he did not seem to see it.

Could he see anything? Yes! Recovering in an instant his steadiness and demeanor, and with a dignity and joy never before seen on his face, he stepped forward to meet his bride. They looked into each other's eyes, and it seemed as if his gaze would never wander from her face.

"At last!" she said. "At last," he echoed solemnly, bowing his head. It was a scene with great dramatic

power, as well as one of great joy. Yet as beautiful as this story is, it is but a mere suggestion of what will actually take place in heaven when Christians, who have been walking through this world of trial and sorrow, "shall see [him] face to face" (1 Corinthians 13:12).
Selected

> Just longing, dear Lord, for you,
> Jesus, beloved and true;
> Yearning and wondering when
> You'll be coming back again,
> Under all I say and do,
> Just longing, dear Lord, for you.
>
> Some glad day, all watching past,
> You will come for me at last;
> Then I'll see you, hear your voice,
> Be with you, with you rejoice;
> How the sweet hope thrills me through,
> Sets me longing, dear Lord, for you.

Willing to Wait in Darkness

> But now, all you who light fires and provide yourselves with flaming torches, go, walk in the light of your fires and of the torches you have set ablaze. This is what you shall receive from my hand: You will lie down in torment.
>
> Isaiah 50:11

This is a solemn warning to those who walk in darkness and who try to help themselves find the light. They are described as the kindling for a fire that is surrounding itself with sparks. What does this mean?

It means that when we are in darkness, the temptation is to find our own way without trusting in the Lord and relying upon Him. Instead of allowing Him to help us, we try to help ourselves. We seek the light of the natural way and the advice of our friends. We reason out our own conclusions and thereby may be tempted to accept a path of deliverance that would not be of God at all.

The light we see may be the fires from our own kindling, or deceptive beacons leading us toward the danger of the rocks. And God will allow us to walk in the false light of those sparks, but the end will be sorrow.

Beloved, never try to get out of a dark place except in God's timing and in His way. A time of trouble and darkness is meant to teach you lessons you desperately need. Premature deliverance may circumvent God's work of grace in your life. Commit the entire situation to Him, and be willing to abide in darkness, knowing He is present.

Remember, it is better to walk in the dark with God than to walk alone in the light. *from* The Still Small Voice

Stop interfering with God's plans and with His will. Touching anything of His mars the work. Moving the hands of a clock to suit you does not change the time. You may be able to rush the unfolding of some aspects of God's will, but you harm His work in the long run. You can force a rosebud open, but you spoil the flower. Leave everything to Him, without exception. "Not what I will, but what you will" (Mark 14:36). *Stephen Merritt*

His Way

God sent me on when I would stay
    ('Twas cool within the wood);
I did not know the reason why.
I heard a boulder crashing by
    'Cross the path where I had stood.

He had me stay when I would go;
    "Your will be done," I said.
They found one day at early dawn,
Across the way I would have gone,
    A serpent with a mangled head.

I ask no more the reason why,
    Although I may not see
The path ahead, His way I go;
For though I know not, He does know,
    And He will choose safe paths for me.

from *Sunday School Times*

Maintaining the Proper Balance

Everything is against me!

Genesis 42:36

All things God works for the good
of those who love him.

Romans 8:28

Many people are lacking when it comes to power. But how is power produced?

The other day, my friend and I were passing by the power plant that produces electricity for the streetcars. We heard the hum and roar of the countless wheels of the turbines, and I asked my friend, "How is the power produced?" He replied, "It simply is generated by the turning of those wheels and the friction they create. The rubbing produces the electric current."

In a similar way, when God desires to create more power in your life, He creates more friction. He uses this pressure to generate spiritual power. Some people cannot handle it and run from the pressure instead of receiving the power and using it to rise above the painful experience that produced it.

Opposition is essential to maintaining true balance between forces. It is the centripetal and centrifugal forces acting in opposition to each other that keep our planet in the proper orbit. The propelling action coupled with the repelling counteraction keep the earth in orbit around the sun instead of flinging it into space and a path of certain destruction.

God guides our lives in the same way. It is not enough to have only a propelling force. We need an equal repelling force, so He holds us back through the testing ordeals of life. The pressures of temptations and trials and all the life changes that seem to be against us further our progress and strengthen our foundation.

Let us thank Him for both the weights and the wings He produces. And realizing we are divinely propelled, let us press on with faith and patience in our high and heavenly calling. *A. B. Simpson*

> In a factory building there are wheels and
> gearings,
> There are cranks, pulleys, belts either tight
> or slack—

Some are whirling swiftly, some are turning
slowly,
Some are thrusting forward, some are
pulling back;
Some are smooth and silent, some are rough
and noisy,
Pounding, rattling, clanking, moving with
a jerk;

In a wild confusion in a seeming chaos,
Lifting, pushing, driving—but they do their
work.
From the mightiest lever to the smallest cog
or gear,
All things move together for the purpose
planned;
And behind the working is a mind
controlling,
And a force directing, and a guiding hand.

So all things are working for the Lord's
beloved;
Some things might be hurtful if alone they
stood;
Some might seem to hinder; some might
draw us backward;

But they work together, and they work for
good,
All the thwarted longings, all the stern
denials,
All the contradictions, hard to understand.
And the force that holds them, speeds them
and retards them,
Stops and starts and guides them—is our
Father's hand.

Annie Johnson Flint

Developing Your Gifts

Tell me what charges you have against me.

Job 10:2

O tested soul, perhaps the Lord is sending you through this trial to develop your gifts. You have some gifts that would never have been discovered if not for trials. Do you not know that your faith never appears as great in the warm summer weather as it does during a cold winter? Your love is all too often like a firefly, showing very little light except when surrounded by darkness. And hope is like the stars — unseen in the sunshine of prosperity and only discovered during a night of adversity. Afflictions are often the dark settings God uses to mount the jewels of His children's gifts, causing them to shine even brighter.

Wasn't it just a short time ago that on your knees you prayed, "Lord, I seem to have no faith. Please show me that I do"? Wasn't your prayer, even though you may not have realized it at the time, actually asking for trials? For how can you know if you have faith, until your faith is exercised? You can depend upon the fact that God often sends trials so our gifts may be discovered and so we may be certain of their existence. And there is more than just discovering our gifts—we experience *real growth in grace* as another result of our trials being sanctified by Him.

God trains His soldiers not in tents of ease and luxury but by causing them to endure lengthy marches and difficult service. He makes them wade across streams, swim through rivers, climb mountains, and walk many tiring miles with heavy backpacks.

Dear Christian, could this not account for the troubles you are now experiencing? Could this not be the reason He is dealing with you? *Charles H. Spurgeon*

Being left alone by Satan is not evidence of being blessed.

Daring to Follow in Faith

By faith Abraham, when called to go to
a place he would later receive as his inheritance,
obeyed and went, even though he did not
know where he was going.

Hebrews 11:8

Abraham "did not know where he was going"—it simply was enough for him to know he went with God. He did not lean as much on the promises as he did on the Promiser. And he did not look at the difficulties of his circumstances but looked to his King—the eternal, limitless, invisible, wise, and only God—who had reached down from His throne to direct his path and who would certainly prove Himself.

O glorious faith! Your works and possibilities are these: contentment to set sail with the orders still sealed, due to unwavering confidence in the wisdom of the Lord High Admiral; and a willingness to get up, leave everything, and follow Christ, because of the joyful assurance that earth's best does not compare with heaven's least. *F. B. Meyer*

In no way is it enough to set out cheerfully with God on any venture of faith. You must also be willing to take your ideas of what the journey will be like and tear them into tiny pieces, for nothing on the itinerary will happen as you expect.

Your Guide will not keep to any beaten path. He will lead you through ways you would never have dreamed your eyes would see. He knows no fear, and He expects you to fear nothing while He is with you.

> The day had gone; alone and weak
> I groped my way within a bleak
>   And sunless land.
> The path that led into the light
> I could not find! In that dark night
>   God took my hand.
>
> He led me that I might not stray,
> And brought me by a safe, new way
>   I had not known.
> By waters still, through pastures green
> I followed Him—the path was clean
>   Of briar and stone.
>
> The heavy darkness lost its strength,
> My waiting eyes beheld at length

The streaking dawn.
On, safely on, through sunrise glow
I walked, my hand in His, and lo,
    The night had gone.

Annie Porter Johnson

Trusting the Stonecutter's Skill

The hand of the LORD has done this.

Job 12:9

A number of years ago the most magnificent diamond in the history of the world was found in an African mine. It was then presented to the king of England to embellish his crown of state. The king sent it to Amsterdam to be cut by an expert stonecutter. Can you imagine what he did with it?

He took this gem of priceless value and cut a notch in it. Then he struck it one hard time with his hammer, and the majestic jewel fell into his hand, broken in two. What recklessness! What wastefulness! What criminal carelessness!

Actually, that is not the case at all. For you see, that one blow with the hammer had been studied and planned for days, and even weeks. Drawings and models had been made of the gem. Its quality, defects, and possible lines along which it would split had all been studied to the smallest detail. And the man to whom it was entrusted was one of the most skilled stonecutters in the world.

Now do you believe that blow was a mistake? No, it was the capstone and the culmination of the stonecutter's skill. When he struck that blow, he did the one thing that would bring that gem to its most perfect shape, radiance, and jeweled splendor. The blow that seemed to be the ruin of the majestic precious stone was actually its perfect redemption, for from the halves were fashioned two magnificent gems. Only the skilled eye of the expert stonecutter could have seen the beauty of two diamonds hidden in the rough, uncut stone as it came from the mine.

Sometimes, in the same way, God lets a stinging blow fall on your life. You bleed, feeling the pain, and your soul cries out in agony. At first you think the blow is an appalling mistake. But it is not, for you are the most precious jewel in the world to God. And He is the most skilled stonecutter in the universe.

Someday you are to be a jewel adorning the crown of the King. As you lie in His hand now, He knows just how to deal with you. Not one blow will be permitted to fall on your apprehensive soul except what the love of God allows. And you may be assured that from the depths of the experience, you will see untold blessings and spiritual enrichment you have never before imagined. *J. H. M.*

In one of George MacDonald's books, one of the characters makes this bitter statement: "I wonder why God made me. I certainly don't see any purpose in it!" Another of the characters responds, "Perhaps you don't see any purpose yet, but then, He isn't finished making you. And besides, you are arguing with the process."

If people would only believe they are still in the process of creation, submit to the Maker, allowing Him to handle them as the potter handles clay, and yield themselves in one shining, deliberate action to the turning of His wheel, they would soon find themselves able to welcome every pressure from His hand on them, even if it results in pain. And sometimes they should not only believe but also have God's purpose in sight: "bringing many sons to glory" (Hebrews 2:10).

> Not a single blow can hit,
> Till the God of love sees fit.

Abandoned to God's
Power and Will

"Not by might nor by power, but by my Spirit,"
says the LORD Almighty.

Zechariah 4:6

Once as I walked along the road on a steep hill, I caught sight of a boy on a bicycle near the bottom. He was pedaling uphill against the wind and was obviously working tremendously hard. Just as he was exerting the greatest effort and painfully doing the best he could do, a streetcar, also going up the hill, approached him. It was not traveling too fast for the boy to grab hold of a rail at the rear, and I am sure you can guess the result. He went up the hill as effortlessly as a bird gliding through the sky.

This thought then flashed through my mind: "I am like that boy on the bicycle in my weariness and weakness. I am pedaling uphill against all kinds of opposition and am almost worn out with the task. But nearby there is great power available—the strength of the Lord Jesus. All I must do is get in touch with Him and maintain communication with Him. And even if I grab hold with only one little finger of faith, it will be enough to make His power mine to accomplish the act of service that now overwhelms me."

Seeing this boy on his bicycle helped me to set aside my weariness and to recognize this great truth. *from* The Life of Fuller Purpose

Abandoned

Utterly abandoned to the Holy Ghost!
Seeking all His fullness, whatever the cost;
Cutting all the moorings, launching in the
deep
Of His mighty power—strong to save and
keep.

Utterly abandoned to the Holy Ghost!
Oh! The sinking, sinking, until self is lost!
Until the emptied vessel lies broken at His
feet;
Waiting till His filling shall make the work
complete.

Utterly abandoned to the will of God;
Seeking for no other path than my Master
trod;
Leaving ease and pleasure, making Him my
choice,
Waiting for His guidance, listening for His
voice.

Utterly abandoned! No will of my own;
For time and for eternity, His, and His
alone;
All my plans and purposes lost in His sweet
will,
Having nothing, yet in Him all things
possessing still.

Utterly abandoned! It's so sweet to be
Captive in His bonds of love, yet wondrously
free;
Free from sin's entanglements, free from
doubt and fear,
Free from every worry, burden, grief, or
care.

Utterly abandoned! Oh, the rest is sweet,
As I tarry, waiting, at His blessed feet;

Waiting for the coming of the Guest divine,
Who my inmost being will perfectly refine.

Lo! He comes and fills me, Holy Spirit
                    sweet!
I, in Him, am satisfied! I, in Him, complete!
And the light within my soul will nevermore
                    grow dim
While I keep my covenant—abandoned
                    unto Him!

                              Author unknown

Walking in His Way

He knows the way that I take.

Job 23:10

O believer, what a glorious assurance this verse is! What confidence I have because "the way that I take"—this way of trials and tears, however winding, hidden, or tangled—"He knows"! When the "furnace [is] heated seven times hotter than usual" (Daniel 3:19), I can know He still lights my way. There is an almighty Guide who knows and directs my steps, whether they lead to the bitter water at the well of Marah or to the joy and refreshment of the oasis at Elim (see Exodus 15:23, 27).

The way is dark to the Egyptians yet has its own pillar of cloud and fire for God's Israel. The furnace may be hot, but not only can I trust the hand that lights the fire, I can also have the assurance the fire will not consume but only refine. And when the refining process is complete, not a moment too soon or too late, "I will come forth as gold" (Job 23:10).

When I feel God is the farthest away, He is often the nearest to me. "When my spirit grows faint within me, it is you who know my way" (Psalm 142:3). Do we know of another who shines brighter than the most radiant sunlight, who meets us in our room with the first waking light, who has an infinitely tender and compassionate watchfulness over us throughout our day, and who "knows the way that [we] take"?

The world, during a time of adversity, speaks of "providence" with a total lack of understanding. They dethrone God, who is the living, guiding Sovereign of the universe, to some inanimate, dead abstraction. What they call "providence" they see as occurrences of fate, reducing God from His position as our acting, powerful, and personal Jehovah.

The pain would be removed from many an agonizing trial if only I could see what Job saw during his time of severe affliction, when all earthly hope lay dashed at his feet. He saw nothing but the hand of God—God's hand behind the swords of the Sabeans who attacked his servants and cattle, and behind the devastating lightning; God's hand giving wings to the mighty desert winds, which swept away his children;

and God's hand in the dreadful silence of his shattered home.

Thus, seeing God in everything, Job could say, "*The LORD* gave and *the LORD* has taken away; may the name of *the LORD* be praised" (Job 1:21, author's italics). Yet his faith reached its zenith when this once-powerful prince of the desert "sat among the ashes" (Job 2:8) and still could say, "Though he slay me, yet will I hope in him" (Job 13:15). *J. R. Macduff*

The Discipline of Faith

Everything is possible for him who believes.

Mark 9:23

The "everything" mentioned here does not always come simply by asking, because God is always seeking to teach you the way of faith. Your training for a life of faith requires many areas of learning, including the trial of faith, the discipline of faith, the patience of faith, and the courage of faith. Often you will pass through many stages before you finally realize the result of faith—namely, the victory of faith.

Genuine moral fiber is developed by enduring the discipline of faith. When you have made your request to God, and the answer still has not come, what are you to do? Keep on believing His Word! Never be swayed from it by what you may see or feel. Then as you stand firm, your power and experience is being developed, strengthened, and deepened. When you remain unswayed from your stance of faith, even in view of supposed contradictions to God's Word, you grow stronger on every front.

God will often purposely delay in giving you His answer, and in fact, the delay is just as much an answer to your prayer as is the fulfillment when it comes. He worked this way in the lives of all the great Bible characters. Abraham, Moses, and Elijah were not great in the beginning but were made great through the discipline of their faith. Only through that discipline were they then equipped for the work to which God had called them.

Think, for example, of Joseph, whom the Lord was training for the throne of Egypt. Psalm 105:19 (KJV) says, "The word of the LORD tried him." It was not the prison life with its hard beds or poor food that "tried him" but "the word of the LORD." The words God spoke into his heart in his early years, concerning his elevated place of honor above his brothers, were the words that were always before him. He remained alone in prison, in spite of his innocence, and watched others being released who were justly incarcerated. Yet he remembered God's words even when every step of his career made fulfillment seem more and more impossible.

These were the times that tried his soul, but they were also the times of his spiritual growth and development. Then, when word of his release from prison finally came, he was found ready and equipped for the delicate task of dealing with his wayward brothers. And he was able to do so with a love and a patience only surpassed by God Himself.

No amount of persecution will try you as much as experiences like these—ones in which you are required to wait on God. Once He has spoken His promise to work, it is truly hard to wait as you see the days go by with no fulfillment. Yet it is this discipline of faith that will bring you into a knowledge of God that would otherwise be impossible.

Instant Obedience

On that very day Abraham [did] ...
as God told him.

Genesis 17:23

Instant obedience is the only kind of obedience there is, for *delayed* obedience is disobedience. Each time God calls upon us to do something, He is offering to make a covenant with us. Our part is to obey, and then He will do His part to send a special blessing.

The only way to be obedient is to obey instantly— *"On that very day,"* as Abraham did. I know we often postpone doing what we know to do, and then later do it as well as we can. Certainly this is better than not doing it at all. By then, however, it is at best only a crippled, disfigured, and partial attempt toward obedience. *Postponed obedience can never bring us the full blessing God intended or what it would have brought had we obeyed at the earliest possible moment.*

What a pity it is how we rob ourselves, as well as

God and others, by our procrastination! Remember, "On that very day" is the Genesis way of saying, "Do it now!" *from* Messages for the Morning Watch

Martin Luther once said, "A true believer will crucify, or put to death, the question, 'Why?' He will simply obey without questioning." And I refuse to be one of those people who "unless ... [I] see miraculous signs and wonders ... will never believe" (John 4:48). I will obey without questioning.

> Ours not to make reply,
>> Ours not to reason why,
> Ours but to do and die.

Obedience is the fruit of faith; patience is the early blossom on the tree of faith. *Christina Rossetti*

Clinging by Faith to God

"I will not let you go unless you bless me." ...
Then he blessed him there.

Genesis 32:26, 29

Jacob won the victory and the blessing here not by wrestling *but by clinging.* His hip was out of joint and he could struggle no longer, but he would not let go. Unable to wrestle further, he locked his arms around the neck of his mysterious opponent, helplessly resting all his weight upon him, until he won at last.

We too will not win the victory in prayer until we cease our struggling. We must give up our own will and throw our arms around our Father's neck in clinging faith.

What can our feeble human strength take by force from the hand of omnipotence? Are we able to wrestle blessings from God by force? Strong-willed violence on our part will never prevail with Him. What wins blessings and victories is the strength of clinging faith.

It is not applying pressure or insisting upon our own will that brings victory. It is won when humility and trust unite in saying, "Not my will, but yours be done" (Luke 22:42).

We are strong with God only to the degree that self is conquered and is dead. Blessings come not by wrestling but by clinging to Him in faith. *J. R. Miller*

An incident from the prayer life of Charles H. Usher illustrates how *"wrestling prayer"* is actually a hindrance to prevailing prayer. He shared this story: "My little boy, Frank, was very ill, and the doctors held out little hope of his recovery. I used all the prayer knowledge I possessed on his behalf, but he continued to worsen. This went on for several weeks.

"One day as I stood watching him while he lay on his bed, I realized he could not live much longer without a quick turn for the better. I said to the Lord, 'Oh, God, I have spent much time in prayer for my son, and yet he is no better. I will now leave him to You and give myself to prayer for others. If it is Your will to take him, I choose Your will—I surrender him entirely to You.'

"I called in my dear wife and told her what I had done. She shed some tears but also handed him over to God. Two days later a godly man came to visit us. He had been very interested in our son, Frank, and had prayed often for him. He told us, 'God has given me faith to believe that your son will recover. Do you have that faith?'

"I responded, 'I have surrendered him to God, but I will now go again to Him regarding my son.' I did just that and while in prayer discovered I had faith for his recovery. From that time forward he began to get better. I then realized that it was the *'wrestling'* of my prayers that had hindered God's answer, and that if I had continued to wrestle, being unwilling to surrender him to God, he would probably not be here today."

O dear child of God, if you want God to answer your prayers, you must be prepared to "walk in the footsteps of the faith that our father Abraham had" (Romans 4:12), even to the mountain of sacrifice.

God's Secret Counsel

Whether you turn to the right or to the left,
your ears will hear a voice behind you, saying,
"This is the way; walk in it."

Isaiah 30:21

When we have doubts or are facing difficulties, when others suggest courses of action that are conflicting, when caution dictates one approach but faith another, we should be still. We should quiet each intruding person, calm ourselves in the sacred stillness of God's presence, study His Word for guidance, and with true devotion focus our attention on Him. We should lift our nature into the pure light radiating from His face, having an eagerness to know only what God our Lord will determine for us. Soon He will reveal by His secret counsel a distinct and unmistakable sense of His direction.

It is unwise for a new believer to depend on this approach alone. He should wait for circumstances to also confirm what God is revealing. Yet Christians who have had many experiences in their walk with Him know the great value of secret fellowship with the Lord as a means of discerning His will.

Are you uncertain about which direction you should go? Take your question to God and receive guidance from either the light of His smile or the cloud of His refusal. You must get alone with Him, where the lights and the darknesses of this world cannot interfere and where the opinions of others cannot reach you. You must also have the courage to wait in silent expectation, even when everyone around you is insisting on an immediate decision or action. If you will do these things, the will of God will become clear to you. And you will have a deeper concept of who He is, having more insight into His nature and His heart of love.

All this will be your unsurpassed gift. It will be a heavenly experience, a precious eternal privilege, and the rich reward for the long hours of waiting. *David*

> "STAND STILL," my soul, for so your Lord
> commands:
> E'en when your way seems blocked, leave it
> in His wise hands;
> His arm is mighty to divide the wave.
> "Stand still," my soul, "stand still" and you
> will see

How God can work the "impossible" for
thee,
For with a great deliverance He does save.

Be not impatient, but in stillness stand,
Even when surrounded on every hand,
In ways your spirit does not comprehend.
God cannot clear your way till you are still,
That He may work in you His blessed will,
And all your heart and will to Him do bend.

"BE STILL," my soul, for just when you are
still,
Can God reveal Himself to you; until
Through you His love and light and life can
freely flow;
In stillness God can work through you and
reach
The souls around you. He then through you
can teach
His lessons, and His power in weakness
show.

"BE STILL"—a deeper step in faith and rest.
"Be still and know" your Father does know
best
The way to lead His child to that fair land,
A "summer" land, where quiet waters flow;

Where longing souls are satisfied, and
"know
Their God," and praise for all that He has
planned.

Selected

Trusting God's Hands — Not Yours

> We do not know what to do,
> but our eyes are upon you.
>
> 2 Chronicles 20:12

An Israelite named Uzzah lost his life because he "reached out and took hold of the ark of God" (2 Samuel 6:6). He placed his hands on it with the best of intentions — to steady it, "because the oxen stumbled" (2 Samuel 6:6) — but nevertheless, he had overstepped his bounds by touching the Lord's work, and "therefore God struck him down" (2 Samuel 6:7). *Living a life of faith often requires us to leave things alone.*

If we have completely entrusted something to God, we must keep our hands off it. He can guard it better than we can, and He does not need our help. "Be still before the LORD and wait patiently for him; do not fret when men succeed in their ways, when they carry out their wicked schemes" (Psalm 37:7).

Things in our lives may seem to be going all wrong, but God knows our circumstances better than we do. And He will work at the perfect moment, if we will completely trust Him to work in His own way and in His own time. Often there is nothing as godly as inactivity on our part, or nothing as harmful as restless working, for God has promised to work His sovereign will. *A. B. Simpson*

Being perplexed, I say,
   "Lord, make it right!
Night is as day to You,
   Darkness as light.
I am afraid to touch
Things that involve so much;
My trembling hand may shake,
My skilless hand may break;
Yours can make no mistake."

Being in doubt I say,
   "Lord, make it plain;
Which is the true, safe way?
   Which would be gain?
I am not wise to know,
Nor sure of foot to go;
What is so clear to Thee,
Lord, make it clear to me!"

It is such a comfort to drip the entanglements and perplexities of life into God's hands and leave them there.

Open and Closed Doors

With skillful hands he led them.

Psalm 78:72

When you are unsure which course to take, totally submit your own judgment to that of the Spirit of God, asking Him to shut every door except the right one. But meanwhile keep moving ahead and consider the absence of a direct indication from God to be the evidence of His will that you are on His path. And as you continue down the long road, you will find that He has gone before you, locking doors you otherwise would have been inclined to enter. Yet you can be sure that somewhere beyond the locked doors is one He has left unlocked. And when you open it and walk through, you will find yourself face-to-face with a turn in the river of opportunity—one that is broader and deeper than anything you ever dared to imagine, even in your wildest dreams. So set sail on it, because it flows to the open sea.

God often guides us through our circumstances. One moment, our way may seem totally blocked, but then suddenly some seemingly trivial incident occurs, appearing as nothing to others but speaking volumes to the keen eye of faith. And sometimes these events are repeated in various ways in response to our prayers. They certainly are not haphazard results of chance but are God opening up the way we should walk, by directing our circumstances. *And they begin to multiply as we advance toward our goal*, just as the lights of a city seem to increase as we speed toward it while traveling at night. *F. B. Meyer*

If you go to God for guidance, He will guide you. But do not expect Him to console you by showing you His list of purposes concerning you, when you have displayed distrust or even half-trust in Him. What He will do, if you will trust Him and go cheerfully ahead when He shows you the way, is to guide you still farther. *Horace Bushnell*

As moves my fragile boat across the storm-
swept sea,
Great waves beat o'er her side, as north
wind blows;

Deep in the darkness hid lie threat'ning
rocks and reefs;
But all of these, and more, my pilot
knows.

Sometimes when darkness falls, and every
light's gone out,
I wonder to what port my frail ship goes;
Although the night be long, and restless all
my hours,
My distant goal, I'm sure, my pilot
knows.

Thomas Curtis Clark

Living in the Center of God's Will

You would have no power over me if it
were not given to you from above.

John 19:11

Nothing that is not part of God's will is allowed to
come into the life of someone who trusts and obeys
Him. This truth should be enough to make our life
one of ceaseless thanksgiving and joy, because God's
will is the most hopeful, pleasant, and glorious thing
in the world. It is the continuous working of His omnipotent power for our benefit, with nothing to pre-
vent it, *if* we remain surrendered and believing.

Someone who was passing through the deep water
of affliction wrote a friend:

> Isn't it glorious to know that no matter how
> unjust something may be, even when it seems
> to have come from Satan himself, *by the time*

it reaches us it is God's will for us and will ultimately work to our good?

"And we know that in all things God works for the good of those who love him" (Romans 8:28). Think of what Christ said even as He was betrayed: *"Shall I not drink the cup the Father has given me?"* (John 18:11, author's italics).

We live fascinating lives if we are living in the center of God's will. All the attacks that Satan hurls at us through the sins of others are not only powerless to harm us but are transformed into blessings along the way. *Hannah Whitall Smith*

> In the center of the circle
>   Of the will of God I stand:
> There can come no second causes,
>   All must come from His dear hand.
> All is well! For it's my Father
>   Who my life has planned.
>
> Shall I pass through waves of sorrow?
>   Then I know it will be best;
> Though I cannot tell the reason,
>   I can trust, and so am blest.
> God is love, and God is faithful.
>   So in perfect Peace I rest.

With the shade and with the sunshine,
  With the joy and with the pain,
Lord, I trust You! Both are needed,
  Each Your wayward child to train,
Earthly loss, if we will know it,
  Often means our heavenly gain.

I. G. W.

Believing God Has Answered

I have faith in God that it will happen
just as he told me.

Acts 27:25

A number of years ago I went to America with a steamship captain who was a very devoted Christian. When we were off the coast of Newfoundland, he said to me, "The last time I sailed here, which was five weeks ago, something happened that revolutionized my entire Christian life. I had been on the bridge for twenty-four straight hours when George Mueller of Bristol, England, who was a passenger on board, came to me and said, 'Captain, I need to tell you that I must be in Quebec on Saturday afternoon.' 'That is impossible,' I replied. 'Very well,' Mueller responded, 'if your ship cannot take me, God will find some other way, for I have never missed an engagement in fifty-seven years. Let's go down to the chartroom to pray.'

"I looked at this man of God and thought to myself,

'What lunatic asylum did he escape from?' I had never encountered someone like this. 'Mr. Mueller,' I said, 'do you realize how dense the fog is?' 'No,' he replied. *'My eye is not on the dense fog but on the living God, who controls every circumstance of my life.'*

"He then knelt down and prayed one of the most simple prayers I've ever heard. When he had finished, I started to pray, but he put his hand on my shoulder and told me *not* to pray. He said, 'First, you do not believe God will answer, and second, I BELIEVE HE HAS. Consequently, there is no need whatsoever for you to pray about it.'

"As I looked at him, he said, 'Captain, I have known my Lord for fifty-seven years, and there has never been even a single day that I have failed to get an audience with the King. Get up, Captain, and open the door, and you will see that the fog is gone.' I got up, and indeed the fog was gone. And on Saturday afternoon George Mueller was in Quebec for his meeting." *Selected*

> If our love were just more simple,
>   We would take Him at His word;
> And our lives would be all sunshine,
>   In the sweetness of our Lord.

Refusing the Shallow Life

> Some [seed] fell on rocky places, where it
> did not have much soil. It sprang up quickly,
> because the soil was shallow.
>
> Matthew 13:5

Shallow! From the context of the teaching of this parable, it seems that we must have something to do with the depth of the soil. The fruitful seed fell on "good soil" (Matthew 13:8), or good and honest hearts. I suppose the shallow people are those who *"did not have much soil"*—those who have no real purpose in life and are easily swayed by a tender appeal, a good sermon, or a simple melody. And at first it seems as if they will amount to something for God, but because they *"[do] not have much soil,"* they have no depth or genuine purpose, and no earnest desire to know His will in order to do it. Therefore we should be careful to maintain the soil of our hearts.

When a Roman soldier was told by his guide that if

he insisted on taking a certain journey, it would probably be fatal, he answered, "It is necessary for me to go — it is not necessary for me to live." That was true depth of conviction, and only when we are likewise convicted will our lives amount to something. But a shallow life lives on its impulses, impressions, intuitions, instincts, and largely on its circumstances. Those with profound character, however, look beyond all these and move steadily ahead, seeing the future, where sorrow, seeming defeat, and failure will be reversed. They sail right through storm clouds into the bright sunshine, which always awaits them on the other side.

Once God has deepened us, He can give us His deepest truths, His most profound secrets, and will trust us with greater power. Lord, lead us into the depths of Your life and save us from a shallow existence!

> On to broader fields of holy vision;
> On to loftier heights of faith and love;
> Onward, upward, apprehending wholly,
> All for which He calls you from above.

> A. B. Simpson

Walking onto the Stage
of This World

In me ... peace.

John 16:33

There is a vast difference between pleasure and blessedness. Paul experienced imprisonment, pain, sacrifice, and suffering to their very limits, yet through it all he was blessed. All the beatitudes became real in his heart and life, *in the midst* of his difficult circumstances.

Paganini, the great Italian violinist, once stepped onstage only to discover there was something wrong with his violin, just as the audience was ending their applause. He looked at the instrument for a moment and suddenly realized it was not his best and most valuable one. In fact, the violin was not his at all. Momentarily he felt paralyzed, but he quickly turned to his audience, telling them there had been some mistake and he did not have his own violin. He stepped back behind the curtain, thinking he must have left it backstage, but discovered that someone had stolen his and left the inferior one in its place.

After remaining behind the curtain for a moment, Paganini stepped onstage again to speak to the audience. He said, "Ladies and Gentlemen, I will now demonstrate to you that the music is not in the instrument but in the soul." Then he played as never before, and beautiful music flowed from that inferior instrument until the audience was so enraptured that their enthusiastic applause nearly lifted the ceiling of the concert hall. He had indeed revealed to them that the music was not in his instrument but in his own soul!

Dear tested and tried believer, it is your mission to walk onto the stage of this world in order to reveal to all of heaven and earth that the music of life lies not in your circumstances or external things but in your own soul.

> If peace be in your heart,
> The wildest winter storm is full of solemn
> beauty,
> The midnight flash but shows your path of
> duty,
> Each living creature tells some new and
> joyous story,

The very trees and stones all catch a ray of
glory,
If peace be in your heart.

Charles Francis Richardson

Waiting for God's Confirmation

The ark of the covenant of the LORD
went before them.

Numbers 10:33

God sometimes does influence us with a simple touch or feeling, but not so we would act on the feeling. If the touch is from Him, He will then provide sufficient evidence to confirm it beyond the slightest doubt.

Consider the beautiful story of Jeremiah, when he felt God leading him to purchase the field at Anathoth. He did not act on his initial feeling but waited for God to completely fulfill His words to him before taking action. Then once his cousin came to him, bringing the external evidence of God's direction by making a proposal for the purchase, he responded and said, *"I knew that this was the word of the LORD"* (Jeremiah 32:8, author's italics).

Jeremiah waited until God confirmed his feeling

through a providential act, and then he worked with a clear view of the facts, which God could also use to bring conviction to others. God wants us to act only once we have His mind on a certain situation. We are not to ignore the Shepherd's personal voice to us, but like "Paul and his companions" (Acts 16:6) at Troas, we are to listen and also examine His providential work in our circumstances, in order to glean the full mind of the Lord. *A. B. Simpson*

Wherever God's finger points, His hand will
clear a way.

Never say in your heart what you will or will not do but wait until God reveals His way to you. As long as that way is hidden, it is clear that there is no need of action and that *He holds Himself accountable for all the results of keeping you exactly where you are. Selected*

For God through ways we have not known,
Will lead His own.

Getting Ready to Move

> Now we know that if the earthly tent we live in is
> destroyed, we have a building from God, an eternal
> house in heaven, not built by human hands.
>
> 2 Corinthians 5:1

The owner of the house I have lived in for many years has notified me that he will do little or nothing to keep it in repair. He also advised me to be ready to move.

At first this was not very welcome news. In many respects the surrounding area is quite pleasant, and if not for the evidence of a somewhat declining condition, the house seems rather nice. Yet a closer look reveals that even a light wind causes it to shake and sway, and its foundation is not sufficient to make it secure. Therefore I am getting ready to move.

As I consider the move, it is strange how quickly my interest is transferred to my prospective new home in another country. I have been consulting maps and studying accounts of its inhabitants. And someone who has come from there to visit has told me that it is beautiful beyond description and that language is inadequate to fully describe what he heard while there. He said that in order to make an investment there, he has suffered the loss of everything he owned here, yet rejoices in what others would call a sacrifice. Another person, whose love for me has been proved by the greatest possible test, now lives there. He has sent me several clusters of the most delicious grapes I have ever eaten, and after tasting them everything here tastes very bland.

Several times I have gone to the edge of the river that forms the boundary between here and there and have longed to be with those singing praises to the King on the other side. Many of my friends have moved across that river, but before leaving here they spoke of my following them later. I have seen the smile on their faces as they passed from my sight. So each time I am asked to make some new investment here, I now respond, "I am getting ready to move." *Selected*

The words of Jesus during His last days on earth vividly express His desire to go "back to the Father" (John 16:28). We, as His people, also have a vision of something far beyond the difficulties and disappointments of this life and are traveling toward fulfillment, completion, and an enriched life. We too are going "to the Father." Much of our new home is still unclear to us, but two things are certain. Our "Father's house" (John 14:2) is our home. And it is in the presence of the Lord. As believers, we know and understand that we are all travelers and not permanent residents of this world. *R. C. Gillie*

The little birds trust God, for they go
singing
From northern woods where autumn
winds have blown,
With joyous faith their unmarked pathway
winging
To summer lands of song, afar, unknown.

Let us go singing, then, and not go crying:
Since we are sure our times are in His
hand,
Why should we weep, and fear, and call it
dying?
It's merely flying to a Summer Land.

Having the Patience to Wait

When the cloud remained ... the Israelites ...
did not set out.

Numbers 9:19

This was the ultimate test of obedience. It was relatively easy to fold up their tents when the fleecy cloud slowly gathered over the tabernacle and began to majestically float ahead of the multitude of the Israelites. Change normally seems pleasant, and the people were excited and interested in the route, the scenery, and the habitat of the next stopping place.

Yet having to wait was another story altogether. "When the cloud remained," however uninviting and sweltering the location, however trying to flesh and blood, however boring and wearisome to those who were impatient, however perilously close their exposure to danger—there was no option but to remain encamped.

The psalmist said, *"I waited patiently for the LORD;*

he turned to me and heard my cry" (Psalm 40:1, author's italics). And what God did for the Old Testament saints, He will do for believers down through the ages, yet He will often keep us waiting. Must we wait when we are face-to-face with a threatening enemy, surrounded by danger and fear, or below an unstable rock? Would this not be the time to fold our tents and leave? Have we not already suffered to the point of total collapse? Can we not exchange the sweltering heat for "green pastures ... [and] quiet waters" (Psalm 23:2)?

When God sends no answer and "the cloud remain[s]," we must wait. Yet we can do so with the full assurance of God's provision of manna, water from the rock, shelter, and protection from our enemies. He never keeps us at our post without assuring us of His presence or sending us daily supplies.

Young person, wait—do not be in such a hurry to make a change! Minister, stay at your post! You must wait where you are until the cloud clearly begins to move. Wait for the Lord to give you His good pleasure! He will not be late! *from* Daily Devotional Commentary

> An hour of waiting!
> Yet there seems such need

To reach that spot sublime!
I long to reach them—but I long far more
  To trust His time!

  "Sit still, My children"—
Yet the heathen die,
  They perish while I stay!
I long to reach them—but I long far more
  To trust His way!

  It's good to get,
It's good indeed to give!
  Yet it is better still—
O'er breadth, through length, down depth,
            up height,
  To trust His will!

                              F. M. N.

Committing and Submitting

> Commit your way to the LORD.
>
> Psalm 37:5

Talk to God about whatever may be pressuring you and then commit the entire matter into His hands. Do this so that you will be free from the confusion, conflicts, and cares that fill the world today. In fact, anytime you are preparing to do something, undergoing some trial, or simply pursuing your normal business, tell the Father about it. Acquaint Him with it; yes, even *burden Him with it*, and you will have put the concerns and cares of the matter behind you. From that point forward, exercise quiet, sweet diligence in your work, recognizing your dependence on Him to carry the matter for you. Commit your cares and yourself with them, as one burden, to your God. *R. Leighton*

> Build a little fence of trust
> Around today;

> Fill the space with loving work
>   And therein stay.
> Look not through the protective rails
>   Upon tomorrow;
> God will help you bear what comes
>   Of joy or sorrow.

Mary Butts

You will find it impossible to "commit your way to the LORD," unless your way has met with His approval. It can only be done through faith, for if there is even the slightest doubt in your heart that His way is not a good one, faith will refuse to have anything to do with it. Also, this committing of your way to Him must be continuous, not just one isolated action. And no matter how unexpected or extraordinary His guidance may seem and no matter how close to the edge of the cliff He may lead you, never snatch the guiding reins from His hands.

Are you willing to submit all your ways to God, allowing Him to pass judgment on them? There is nothing a Christian needs to more closely examine than his own confirmed views and habits, for we are so prone to taking God's divine approval of them for granted. And that is why some Christians are so anxious and fearful. They have obviously not truly committed their way to the Lord and *left it with Him*. They took it to Him but walked away with it again. *Selected*

Obeying by Faith — Not Sight

You will see neither wind nor rain,
yet this valley will be filled with water, and you,
your cattle and your other animals will drink.
This is an easy thing in the eyes of the LORD;
he will also hand Moab over to you.

2 Kings 3:17 – 18

To human reason, what God was promising seemed simply impossible, but nothing is too difficult for Him. Without any sound or sign and from sources invisible and seemingly impossible, the water flowed the entire night, and "the next morning ... there it was ...! And the land was filled with water.... The sun was shining on the water.... [And it] looked red—like blood" (2 Kings 3:20, 22).

Our unbelief is always desiring some *outward sign*, and the faith of many people is largely based on sensationalism. They are not convinced of the genuineness of God's promises without some visible manifestation.

But the greatest triumph of a person's faith is to "be still, and know that [He is] God" (Psalm 46:10).

The greatest victory of faith is to stand at the shore of the impassable Red Sea and to hear the Master say, *"Stand firm and you will see the deliverance the LORD will bring you today"* (Exodus 14:13, author's italics), and *"Move on"* (Exodus 14:15). As we step out in faith, without any sign or sound, taking our first steps into the water, we will see the water divide. Continuing to march ahead, we will see a pathway open through the very midst of the sea.

Whenever I have seen God's wondrous work in the case of some miraculous healing or some extraordinary deliverance by His providence, the thing that has always impressed me most was the absolute quietness in which it was done. I have also been impressed by the absence of anything sensational and dramatic, and the utter sense of my own uselessness as I stood in the presence of this mighty God, realizing how easy all this was for Him to do without even the faintest effort on His part, or the slightest help from me.

It is the role of faith not to *question* but to simply *obey*. In the above story from Scripture, the people were asked to "make this valley full of ditches" (2 Kings 3:16). The people obeyed, and then water came pouring in from some supernatural source to fill them. What a lesson for our faith!

Are you desiring some spiritual blessing? Then dig the ditches and God will fill them. But He will do this in the most unexpected *places* and in the most unexpected *ways.* May the Lord grant us the kind of faith that acts "by faith, not by sight" (2 Corinthians 5:7), and may we expect Him to work although we see no wind or rain. *A. B. Simpson*

Finishing Well

I am already being poured out like a drink offering,
and the time has come for my departure. I have
fought the good fight, I have finished the race,
I have kept the faith.

2 Timothy 4:6–7

Just as old soldiers compare their battle scars and stories of war when they get together, when we arrive at our heavenly home, we will tell of the goodness and faithfulness of God, who brought us through every trial along the way. I would not like to stand with the multitude clothed in robes made "white in the blood of the Lamb" (Revelation 7:14) and hear these words: " 'These are they who have come out of the great tribulation' — *all except you.*"

How would *you* like to stand there and be pointed out as the only saint who never experienced sorrow? Never! You would feel like a stranger in the midst of a sacred fellowship. Therefore may we be content to share in the battle, for we will soon wear a crown of reward and wave a palm branch of praise. *Charles H. Spurgeon*

During the American Civil War, at the battle of Lookout Mountain, Tennessee, a surgeon asked a soldier where he was hurt. The wounded soldier answered, *"Right near the top of the mountain."* He was not thinking of his gaping wound but was only remembering that he had won the ground near the top of the mountain.

May we also go forth to higher endeavors for Christ, never resting until we can shout from the mountaintop, "I have fought the good fight, I have finished the race, I have kept the faith."

> Finish your work, then rest,
>   Till then rest never;
> Since rest for you with God
>   Is rest forever.

God will examine your life not for medals, diplomas, or degrees but for battle scars.

A medieval singer once sang of his hero:

> With his trusty sword for aid;
>   Ornament it carried none,
> But the notches on the blade.

What nobler medal of honor could any godly person seek than the scars of service, personal loss for the crown of reward, disgrace for the sake of Christ, and being worn out in the Master's service!

Contentment—
Even When Waiting

Sit here while I go over there and pray.

Matthew 26:36

It is a very difficult thing to be kept in the background during a time of crisis. In the garden of Gethsemane, eight of the eleven remaining disciples were left behind to do nothing. When Jesus went ahead to pray, Peter, James, and John went with Him to watch, but the rest sat down to wait. I believe that the ones left behind must have complained. They were *in* the garden, but that was all, for they had no part in the cultivation of its flowers. It was a stormy time of crisis and great stress, yet they were not allowed to participate.

You and I have certainly had that experience and felt the same disappointment. Perhaps you have seen a great opportunity for Christian service arise, and some people are sent immediately to the work, while still others are being trained to go. Yet *you* are forced to do nothing but sit and wait. Or perhaps sickness and poverty has come your way, or you have had to endure some terrible disgrace. Whatever your situation, you have been kept from service, and now you feel angry and do not understand why you should be excluded from this part of the Christian life. It seems unjust that you have been allowed to enter the garden but have found no path assigned to you once inside.

Be still, dear soul — things are not what they seem! You are *not* excluded from any part of the Christian life. Do you believe that the garden of the Lord only has places for those who walk or those who stand? No! It also has a place set apart for those who are compelled to *sit*. Just as there are three voices in a verb — active, passive, and neutral — there are three voices in Christ's verb "live." There are active people, who go straight to the battle, and struggle till the setting of the sun. There are passive people, who stand in the middle and simply report the progress of the fight. Yet there are also neuter people — those who can neither fight nor be spectators of the fight but must simply lie down and wait.

When this experience comes, do not think that you have been turned aside. Remember, it is *Christ Himself* who says to you, "Sit here." *Your* place in the garden has *also* been set apart. God has selected it especially for you, and it is not simply a place of waiting. There are some lives He brings into this world neither to do great work nor to bear great burdens. Their job is simply to be—they are the neuter verbs, or the flowers in the garden that have no active mission. They have won no major victories and have never been honored with the best seats at a banquet—they have simply escaped the sight of people like Peter, James, and John.

However, *Jesus* is delighted by the sight of them, for through their mere fragrance and beauty, they have brought Him joy. And just their existence and the preservation of their loveliness in the valley have lifted the Master's heart. So you need not complain if you are one of these flowers! *Selected*

Streams in the Desert® for Graduates

366 Daily Devotional Readings

L. B. Cowman,
Edited by Jim Reimann

For years, the beloved classic devotional *Streams in the Desert®* has sustained and replenished God's weary desert travelers. Now, bursting forth like a sparkling clear river of wisdom, encouragement, and inspiration, this updated edition of *Streams in the Desert* promises to revive and refresh today's generation of faithful sojourners, providing daily Scripture passages from the popular New International Version and modern, easy-to-understand language that beautifully captures the timeless essence of the original devotional.

Now in mass market size, *Streams in the Desert* comes with two different cover designs. One is ideal for giving to graduates. Both pack away easily for traveling, hiking, hospital visits, or any situation where convenience counts.

Mass Market: 978-0-310-28276-1

Pick up a copy today at your favorite bookstore!

ZONDERVAN®
.com

Leadership Secrets of Billy Graham for Graduates

*Harold Myra and
Marshall Shelley*

Graduation—a time of great excitement and great challenge. A time to be the head of the class, to lead. Give the graduate a look into the leadership secrets of one of the most renowned leaders today, Billy Graham. Filled with devotions and Scriptures to challenge the new graduate, this book is sure to be the perfect gift.

Hardcover: 978-0-310-81217-3

Pick up a copy today at your favorite bookstore!

Streams in the Desert®

366 Daily Devotional Readings

L. B. Cowman. Edited by Jim Reimann, Editor of
My Utmost for His Highest, Updated Edition

For years, the beloved classic devotional *Streams in the Desert* has sustained and replenished God's weary desert travelers. Now, bursting forth like a sparkling clear river of wisdom, encouragement, and inspiration, this updated edition of *Streams in the Desert* promises to revive and refresh today's generation of faithful sojourners, providing daily Scripture passages from the popular, readable New International Version — and modern, easy-to-understand language that beautifully captures the timeless essence of the original devotional.

> I said, "The desert is so wide!"
> I said, "The desert is so bare!"
> What springs the quench my thirst are there?
> Where will I from the tempest hide?

In a barren wilderness, L. B. Cowman long ago dis-covered a fountain that sustained her, and she shared it with the world. *Streams in the Desert* — her collection of prayerful meditations, Christian writings, and God's writ-ten promises — has become one of the most dearly loved, best-selling devotionals of all time since its first publica-tion in 1925. Filled with insight into the richness of God's provision and the purpose of his plan, this enduring classic has encouraged and inspired generations of Christians.

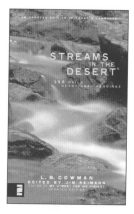

> I heard the flow of hidden
> springs;
> Before me palms rose green
> and fair;
> The birds were singing; all the
> air
> Was filled and stirred with
> angels' wings.

Now Jim Reimann, editor of the highly acclaimed, updated edition of *My Utmost for His Highest* by Oswald Chambers, again brings us the wisdom of the past in the language of today by introducing this updated edition of *Streams in the Desert*. With fresh, contemporary wording and precise NIV text, the timeless message of the original flows unhindered through these pages, lending guidance and hope to a new generation of believers.

Day by day, *Streams in the Desert* will lead you from life's dry, desolate places to the waters of the River of Life—and beyond, to their very Source.

Softcover: 978-0-310-23011-3

Pick up a copy today at your favorite bookstore!

ZONDERVAN®
.com

We want to hear from you. Please send your comments about this book to us in care of zreview@zondervan.com. Thank you.

ZONDERVAN.com/
AUTHORTRACKER
follow your favorite authors